FIRST AID

FOR A WOUNDED MARRIAGE

D1452820

By: Marilyn Phillipps

PREFACE

My husband, Michael, and I have a marriage healed by the power of Jesus. Just a few years ago we had reached the point of divorce and Michael was making plans to marry someone else. Counselors offered no hope, our pastor was resigned to the fact that the marriage was dead, and other Christians advised me to pick up the pieces and get on with my life.

This turmoil initiated a time of training in my life during which I learned the true steadfastness and power of the Lord. When God's Word makes a statement, God is prepared to back it with might and power. The Word would not state "let no man put asunder" without the power of God being able to restore and heal marriages. The Holy Spirit led me step by step in a stand for our marriage and Jesus proved once again that there is nothing impossible with Him. Our marriage was restored and healed by the power of God and the authority of His Word.

The purpose of this book is not to give you in-depth teaching on standing for the healing of your marriage. It is designed, as the title says, to give you first aid for the initial trauma. You will need to seek out the support of your pastor and others to stand in agreement with you. There are also support groups specifically called of God to help you during this time. More information on these groups can be obtained by calling 1-918-743-0365.

This book was written for you. Do not give up hope. Do not become weary in well doing. Know that God is no respecter of persons. What He did for us, He longs to do for you also.

In Jesus,

Marilyn Phillipps

FOREWORD

Just a few years ago nobody looking at the circumstances of our marriage, and especially looking at the kind of man I was, would ever have dreamed that some day I would be writing a foreword to a marriage healing booklet. I was so set in my desire to get out of an awful marriage. I was so put out with the fact that I was saddled with two children and another on the way. I was so in love (or lust) with another woman (Marilyn's best friend) who "understood" me. I was driven by the lust for money. I was trapped by pornography and alcohol. I was self-seeking, self-centered, and selfish. I had made a god out of who I was and what I wanted.

Look at what kind of man is described in 2 Timothy 3:2-5 (NIV). *"People will be lovers of themselves, lovers of money, boastful, proud, abusive, disobedient to their parents, ungrateful, unholy, without love, unforgiving, slanderous, without self-control, brutal, not lovers of the good, treacherous, rash, conceited, lovers of pleasure rather than lovers of God--having a form of godliness but denying its power. Have nothing to do with them."* That is a description of the man that I was.

But...Praise the Lord that we have a God that is a God of FAITH. Praise the Lord that those who serve Him can have His faith. They can see with eyes of faith and not natural eyes. His vision for me (and all mankind) was so different from what I was. It was His desire that I be a man of God, the kind described in His Word. 1 Timothy 3:2-4 (NIV) speaks of a godly man who *"...must be above reproach, the husband of but one wife, temperate, self-controlled, respectable, hospitable, able to teach, not given to drunkenness, manage his own family well and see that his children obey him with proper respect."* In addition He wanted Marilyn , who was in covenant relationship with Him, and me to have the kind of relationship that Adam and Eve had before the fall, to have the kind of relationship that is described in Jeremiah 32:38-41, that our marriage should be of one heart and one way so that we might be blessed by Him and be planted and bearing fruit in this world.

It seems like it would have been so much easier for Marilyn to look at the circumstances. It seems that she would have been better off protecting herself by looking out for herself. But that is not the Lord's way. The essence of what He said to her was that if she would sell out to Him and His Word, there would be nothing preventing her from receiving all of the covenant blessings promised in His Word.

She did sell out to Him and His Word and not to the world's way of doing things. For three hard, long years, in the face of very little encouragement from even the Christian community and certainly none from me, she stood and battled for the Lord's will in her life. It was not an easy battle; in fact she blew it on occasion, but she had a heart after God. This booklet will give you an idea of the battle that you face. But greater is He (the Lord) that is in you than he that is in the world. The victory is yours. To the victor goes the spoils. And in the case of Marilyn's victory, she now has a husband (me) that is serving the Lord and growing in a marriage that's doing honor and service to the Lord.

This statement is going to be strange coming from me but understand it. Marilyn had a tremendously tough fight BUT it was worth it. I was worth it, our marriage was worth it. Don't let the devil rob, steal and kill your marriage. You and your spouse have a godly purpose for your marriage, that it be a powerful tool for the present with its disaster, but rather look to God's heart and vision for what it will be *"...exceeding abundantly above all that we ask or think" Ephesians 3:20.*

Mike

Michael Phillipps

P.S. Marilyn, I love you and thank you so much for standing steadfast despite all of the circumstances for the healing of our marriage.

TABLE OF CONTENTS

— 1 —
Shock

When Michael first informed me that he had found someone else and wanted a divorce, I was in shock. I couldn't think, I couldn't feel. I was numb.

I had known things were not right between us but I had always thought we would work it out. After all, we loved each other. We were married. Things would get better tomorrow.

Suddenly, though, things were never going to get better. He was leaving and did not want to work on the marriage. He said he didn't love me and never had. He said he didn't want the children and never had. I was pregnant with our third child at the time and I felt betrayed and trapped. I remember sitting on the edge of the tub one night crying so hard I thought my body would shake apart. Everything was black and hopeless.

Michael wouldn't go for counseling. He wouldn't talk. All he wanted to do was spend time with her. I felt abandoned and worthless. This wasn't helped by "friends" telling me to get out of the way and let them be happy together.

I went to our pastor and he told me there was nothing that could be done. He said it was a sad situation but that I needed to accept the inevitable. Michael finally agreed to see a counselor because someone told him it would go better in divorce court if he had that on his record. After one session the counselor recommended we get a quick divorce and save time and money. He said we were too far gone for help.

Then I went to a friend of ours whom I knew was serving the Lord mightily. If anyone knew what the Bible had to say, he would. He told me that God would honor the divorce because Michael had been in adultery. He said he didn't know of anything that could be done to stop the break up of the marriage if Michael was unwilling to co-operate.

Finally I went to Jesus. Funny how we take so long to end up where we should have been in the first place.

Jesus met me in the midst of my pain and my tears. He comforted me and loved me and then began to take a very firm stand with me. He showed me plainly from His Word what His standard is regarding marriage. He cut through the emotions of the moment and taught me truth.

That is what this book is all about — TRUTH. If you want sympathy and tears, you will find them readily. People will cry with you and for you quite easily. If you want justification for unforgiveness, you will easily find that also. There are many others who have been hurt and will side with you in your bitterness. If you want the plain and simple truth, though, only the Word of God can give that to you. It may be hard to take at first, but Jesus has promised, *"You shall know the truth and the truth shall set you free"* John 8:32 NIV.

There is power in truth. There is healing in truth. There is restoration in truth. Understand this now, this very minute, **JESUS WANTS YOUR MARRIAGE HEALED.**

If you are reading this book I will assume that you realize that your marriage is in trouble. Perhaps you too are in shock. You never thought this would happen to you. You never believed it was possible. You need help.

First of all, bottom line, no way around it — you need Jesus. If you think you will be able to see your marriage healed without His power, you are mistaken. Without Jesus marriages can only be glued back together. They will always have a major flaw which will give under pressure. Jesus is the only one who can heal a marriage so that the breaking point is not even noticeable. In fact, with Jesus, that which was weakest becomes the strongest. There is no flaw that remains to give under pressure.

Jesus loves you. Just as you are. You don't have to get cleaned up for Him to accept you. You don't have to be good and earn points with Him to get close to Him. He died for you when you were still a sinner. He knows you better than anyone else does, even better than you know yourself. You can't fake Him out. You can't pretend with Him. He knows your heart.

Right now you need to turn to Him and surrender your life to Him. Only He can cleanse you of your sin and get your life in order. You can't do it for yourself. If you could you wouldn't be in the mess your in right now. He is the only one who can fix it.

Pray this prayer right now and give your heart to Him.

"Jesus, I'm hurting. I've been rejected and I feel worthless. I've tried to change on my own and I can't do it. I'm tired of making excuses, tired of trying. I acknowledge to You that I am a sinner. I cannot cleanse myself and I cannot make my life right on my own. I surrender my life to You, Jesus. I receive You as my Lord and my Savior. I accept the cleansing of Your blood for my sins. I let You take over my life right now. Help me, Lord. Comfort me. Teach me. I need

You more than I ever have before. I am Your child, Father."

If you have prayed this prayer really meaning what you are saying, you are now born-again by the Spirit of God. This means that the old nature, the one you were born with, was replaced with a new nature, God's nature. You are going to need that nature to stand for the healing of your marriage. You cannot do it on your power. You must do it by His power.

God has written a very special love letter to His children. It contains instructions for every aspect of life on this earth, for every situation. In His love letter, God has expressed His will for you and has given instruction on how to achieve it. His love letter is the Bible.

In the past you may have tried to read the Bible and it all seemed like Greek to you. That's because you were reading someone else's mail. Now you are a born-again child of God and the letter is written to you. You will now understand what He is saying because His Spirit lives within you and will teach you all things. If you have just now received Jesus for the first time, there is much you must learn. Do not become overwhelmed. God knows you are new at this. He will lead you gently.

Even if you have known the Lord for some time now, you still have some work ahead of you. You are in an all out battle for your home and family. This is going to be work. It is not a passive thing but a very active one. You are going to learn what it means to be a soldier in the Lord's army. This is hand to hand combat but, praise the Lord, He has equipped His children to fight.

You need to realize that your enemy, Satan, and his forces desire to destroy your home. They are using circumstances and people. It is important to know:

PEOPLE ARE NOT YOUR ENEMY.

CIRCUMSTANCES ARE NOT THE PROBLEM.

DO NOT GIVE ULTIMATUMS.

Satan is the master of circumstances. Do not use his tools to attempt to win a victory. If you make demands based on circumstances, ("If you don't stop this, I'm going to leave you") he will manipulate circumstances to make sure you get a chance to fulfill your threat. Ultimatums just set up circumstances to force you into ungodly results. There are many people divorced today who never intended to be but they painted themselves into a corner with the words of their mouths.

Satan fights dirty. He knows what will hurt you the most and he is using those things to wound you. The one you love the most, your spouse, is doing and saying terrible things right now. **YOUR SPOUSE IS NOT YOUR ENEMY**. Remember that. Your spouse is being used of the enemy to destroy your home. I don't care if your spouse is a Christian and has twenty Bible verses to explain what he or she is doing. **IT IS NOT GOD'S WILL FOR YOUR MARRIAGE TO BREAK UP.**

Never mind what people are saying. What is God saying? What does the Bible say?

Never mind what people are doing. What is God doing? What does the Bible say for you to do?

Your home is under enemy attack. If you are going to survive the attack you must know what is happening and how to combat it. The next chapter will help you.

"Jesus, I know our home is under enemy attack. I need Your help. I don't know how to fight. I don't know what to do. I surrender this battle to You. Teach me, help me. I will trust You to do it. Amen."

Diagnosis

Why is all this happening? Why you? Why your marriage? What did you do or not do to cause this?

To understand the crisis in your home, you need to understand some basic principles from God's Word, the Bible. When God first created man and woman He joined them together in marriage, a covenant relationship. To understand marriage as God sees it, we must understand covenant as God sees it.

A covenant is a pact or agreement between two people that binds them in deep, lasting relationship. It really means they are no longer two separate lives but now share one life together. In the Bible we see that God made covenants with several people, a very notable one being the covenant He made with Abraham establishing the Jewish nation (Genesis 12:1-3). Since Jesus' death and resurrection, those who receive Jesus as their Lord and Savior are partners in the New Covenant with God (Hebrews 8:6-13).

Covenant love is strong. It says, "I lay down my life for you" (1 Corinthians 13:1-8). Throughout scripture we see that God remained faithful to His covenant promises even when, man, His covenant partner failed to keep his end of the bargain. Covenant love is faithful regardless of what the other partner is doing. The reason for this is that every covenant contains within it promises and terms or conditions. When people enter into covenant they promise certain things to each other and state the conditions under which they will keep their promise. If one covenant partner is unfaithful to the promises, it does not cause the other one to be also. Throughout the Old Testament we see God, the faithful covenant partner, calling to Israel, the unfaithful covenant partner. Israel's unfaithfulness did not change God's heart toward her. He continues to stand for her, to love her, and to call her back to Him to this day.

The Bible calls marriage a covenant relationship. ("...*though she is your partner, the wife of your marriage covenant*" Malachi 2:14). When you married you entered into a covenant. As part of the ceremony you and your spouse made certain promises to each other. The words differ from ceremony to ceremony but they usually include something like "love, honor, cherish, obey", etc. And your ceremony included certain terms.

For instance, "for better or for worse; for richer, for poorer; in sickness and in health." And the promises and terms probably concluded with the words, "...until death do us part." We call these wedding vows. The Bible has something to say about vows. *"When you vow a vow to God, do not delay in fulfilling it. He has no pleasure in fools; fulfill your vow. It is better not to vow than to make a vow and not fulfill it"* Ecclesiastes 5:4,5 NIV.

Most of us didn't know anything about all of this when we married. We were usually so nervous we didn't know what we were saying anyway. But God was listening. I remember shortly after our marriage was healed a friend of mine was complimenting me on what a fine job I had done in standing for the healing of our marriage. As I listened to her, I got to thinking how wonderful I was and all that I had suffered. I decided God must have been pretty proud to have me on His team. After all, I thought, how many others would have been that faithful to His Word. On the way home from her house, the Lord spoke to my heart very softly and said, "What did you do in standing for your marriage that you didn't promise you would do on your wedding day?"

Suddenly I realized that God had been listening on our wedding day, long before we even knew Him, and He had taken note of what we said. When the "for worse" part came, He was faithful to His commitment to our marriage and He had expected us to be also. It seems so unusual in this day of instant marriage and instant divorce to take a stand for marriage, but by God's standard it's not unusual at all. It is the expected norm.

In the last chapter, I mentioned that we could find no encouragement for healing from our pastor or from counselors. Even our friend who was born-again, Spirit-filled, and serving the Lord mightily believed God had declared the marriage dead because of the adultery. God had a different standard, though. As I returned home from receiving that final counsel I was preparing for the divorce which seemed inevitable. My human love for my husband had died from the constant wounding it had received. I figured if God knew this marriage was dead and gone and He was going to bring me a new husband, I had better just go with the flow and get it over with.

When we have received Jesus as Lord and Savior, though, He has taken up residence within us and He speaks to our hearts according to His Word. I have never heard an audible voice of God, but I have no trouble knowing when He is speaking to me from within. That day He took me to a scripture that I didn't ever remember reading before. *"Now to the married I give this command (not I, but the Lord): A wife must not separate from her husband. But if she does, she must remain unmarried or else be reconciled to her husband. And a husband must not divorce his wife"* (1 Corinthians 7:10,11 NIV).

I was stunned as I looked at that scripture. I couldn't believe God was being so hard about this whole thing. Immediately I turned to the scriptures I had been given by our friend that gave me an "out" to divorce and remarry. I showed them to the Lord and asked Him what He thought about that. He gently took me back to 1 Corinthians 7:10,11 and had me read it again. Slowly it began to sink into me that God wasn't playing games. This thing was for keeps. He had made the rules and He was now enforcing them. I felt a bit upset that He didn't seem to have the same rules for everyone. I pointed out to Him how many Christians I knew who had divorced and remarried and asked Him what about them. Again He did not comment but gently drew me back to 1 Corinthians 7:10,11. He said to me, "This is My standard. You have a choice and I will meet you at whichever one you choose. If you choose to remain single, I will be your husband. I will care for your children as their father. You will never lack for anything nor will they be lacking. I will provide for you as no earthly husband ever could. If you should choose to reconcile, however, I will bring you through to victory."

Immediately I thought of the scriptures, *"Do not be afraid; you will not suffer shame. Do not fear disgrace; you will not be humiliated. You will forget the shame of your youth and remember no more the reproach of your widowhood. For your Maker is your Husband-the Lord Almighty is his name-the Holy One of Israel is your Redeemer; he is called the God of all the earth. The Lord will call you back as if you were a wife deserted and distressed in spirit—a wife who married young, only to be rejected"* (Isaiah 54:4-6 NIV) and *"A father to the fatherless, a defender of widows, is God in his holy dwelling"* (Psalm 68:5 NIV). I knew He meant what He was saying.

The choice did not take me long. I did not want to remain single. I had two children and a third on the way. I wanted a home with a husband and father. I wanted our marriage. I told the Lord, "I want to reconcile, Lord, but I don't know how. I can't even find anyone who will tell me it's possible."

"I say it is possible," was His only answer. "And I will teach you how."

Your marriage is a covenant relationship, the earthly reflection of God's eternal covenant love. Satan hates the unity and power of covenant and is seeking to destroy every marriage he can get (John 10:10). What you have done or not done may have contributed to the downfall of your marriage, but it is not the cause of it. Your marriage has been targeted for destruction by Satan and his forces. The circumstances that you face are just his means of warfare. The name of Jesus is still the name above all names. What is the name of the circumstance you face today? Adultery? Alcoholism? Homosexuality? Incest? Whatever its name is, that name is under the name of Jesus. And scripture says that everything must bow to the name of Jesus. *"Therefore God exalted him to the highest place and gave him the name that is above every name, that at the name of Jesus every knee should bow, in heaven and on earth and under the earth, and every tongue confess that Jesus Christ is Lord, to the glory of God the Father"* (Philippians 2:9-11 NIV).

THE DEVIL'S CHIEF TACTIC IS GOING TO BE TO TRY TO CONVINCE YOU THAT THIS ONE IS TOO BIG FOR GOD. It's a lie! You are in covenant with God through the blood of Jesus and you are standing for a God-ordained covenant relationship on this earth. What power does hell have against that?

Now just as you read that last statement, the enemy said to you, "But what if this marriage isn't God-ordained? What if God doesn't want it healed? Maybe it never was a case of '*what God has joined together.*' If God were for this, would it be this bad?"

Just remember this, God is the originator of marriage. When a couple chooses marriage, they choose God's plan. From the moment they are married, God is committed to working with them to make that plan succeed. *"What God has joined together"* does not just mean those He has told to marry each other. That is the very best way, it is being right in the center of God's will, but few seek Him diligently for a spouse. Many couples, ourselves included, married through their own desire and God had nothing to do with it. That doesn't change His commitment to covenant love and faithfulness, however. It is

God's will for all individuals to be in covenant with Him and for all marriages to be based on Him. When these conditions are not so, He is still 100% for the couple and for the marriage. To end a marriage by saying God wasn't in it is just as wrong as to abort a pregnancy because the child wasn't planned. Once you are in a covenant relationship, allow God to teach you how to bring it forth to fullness in Him. God is faithful to those in covenant with Him even when we fail Him. His desire for us is to learn to be faithful even when our spouse fails us.

"Lord Jesus, teach me what covenant means. Teach me to remain strong and faithful to my word even when my spouse is not. I want to know your heart regarding covenant. I want to see our marriage as you see it. My own love is so wounded right now, Jesus. I cannot do this alone. I don't feel very loving or very giving right now. Please help me, Lord. I will rest in you."

—3—
Pain

Y ou are hurting right now — hurting so badly you don't know if you will ever stop hurting. I know, I have felt that pain. Let me assure you, though, that the pain will stop. When Jesus heals, He does a thorough job.

One day when I was calling out to God from the midst of my pain, Jesus took me through scripture to the Garden of Gethsemane with Him (Mark 14:32-42). For the first time I saw the pain that He had suffered there. At a time when He so desperately needed the love and comfort of another human being, His apostles could not even stay awake. They did not understand His pain, nor did they care. They had had a big meal and it was late and they wanted to sleep.

Does it seem to you that no one knows how you feel right now? Does it seem that no one knows what you are going through? Jesus does. He has felt your loneliness, your rejection, your pain. He has carried it within Himself that you might not have to. He was in such agony that His sweat fell as drops of blood to the ground. He went without comfort that you might be comforted. Let Him comfort you now. Psalm 144, verse 2 says that the Lord is *"my steadfast love and my fortress, my high tower and my deliverer, my shield and He in whom I trust and take refuge"* (Amplified). Right now turn to Him. Let Him be your refuge, your fortress, your shield. He loves you so very much. Only He can truly understand the pain you are feeling. Let Him comfort you.

Jesus showed me something else that happened to Him in that Garden. He was betrayed by someone He loved very much and He was betrayed in the name of love, with a kiss (Matthew 26:47-50). The one you love very much has betrayed you also. Jesus knows how you feel. He has experienced the humiliation and the shame. He has already borne all of this Himself so that you don't have to. When He went to the cross He not only took all your sin there with Him but He also took all your pain, humiliation and shame, and betrayal. Hebrews 12:2,3 says, *"Let us fix our eyes on Jesus, the author and perfecter of our faith, who for the joy set before him endured the cross, scorning its shame, and sat down at the right hand of the throne of God. Consider him who endured such opposition from sinful men, so that you will not grow weary and lose heart."*

When the Holy Spirit inspired Paul to write those words, He had you in mind. He knew then the pain you would feel today. He knew the shame of rejection you would feel. He wants you to look to Jesus. That's why those words have been written, that you might know what to do when this hour came in your life.

Before you can even attempt to stand for the healing of your marriage, you need to allow Jesus to comfort and begin healing you. Begin to read the psalms. David knew pain and rejection. He also knew from Whom his help came. Read how he cried out to the Lord and then how he praised His name even in the midst of his troubles.

Praise is a very effective means of healing. You cannot praise the Lord with your whole heart and stay wounded. At first it will truly be a sacrifice of praise (Hebrews 13:15), you will not feel like doing it. Once you discipline yourself to begin, though, you will find that you draw into the very presence of the Lord and your healing will begin.

Staying in Jesus' presence is the key to healing. Praise Him for Who He is and what He has done. Get your eyes off your problems and circumstances and onto Jesus. Get to know Him like you never have before. Begin to see this as a special time in your life in which you can draw closer and closer to Him.

One of the things that happened during my stand for my husband and our marriage was that I got to know Jesus in a way that I might never had if I had not been forced by circumstances to rely on Him totally. I came to know His immense love for me, His steadfastness, His never-changing heart. He became my Rock in the midst of the storm. No one can ever take from me the love relationship that we developed during those times of turmoil. I know Jesus today in such a deeper way in a time of peace because I got to know Him well in a time of trouble.

Draw close to Jesus. Press in to know Him as you never have before. See this time as an opportunity, not a problem. Allow Jesus to comfort and heal you. He has already borne your pain within Him when He went to the cross for you. You need not carry it now. Give it to Him and allow Him to resurrect you with His healing power. *"For I will restore health to you, and I will heal your wounds, says the Lord; because they have called you an outcast, saying, This is Zion, whom no one seeks after and for whom no one cares!"* (Jeremiah 30:17 Amplified).

Praise the Lord for Who He is and what He has done. Sacrifice praise to Him from the midst of your pain and healing will begin within you. Spend time reading the Bible and ask Jesus to speak to you through His Word. The psalms are a good place to start. See how David rejoiced in the Lord and found comfort in Him even in the midst of heavy trials.

"Jesus, You know I am hurting. You once felt this pain within Yourself. You know the pain of rejection, the shame and humiliation. You took them to the cross for me and now I give them to You. I praise You, Lord! I praise Your Name! I will spend time with You in Your Word. Comfort and heal me, Jesus. Amen."

—4—
Pressure

You are engaged in an awesome conflict. Up until now you have believed that the conflict was between you and your spouse. It is not. It is a conflict between two kingdoms. The kingdom of Satan is warring against the kingdom of God for your spouse and your marriage. God has plans for your spouse. He has plans for your marriage. *"For I know the plans I have for you," says the Lord, "plans to prosper you and not to harm you, plans to give you hope and a future"* (Jeremiah 29:11 NIV).

Your enemy, the devil, also has plans for your spouse. *"Be self-controlled and alert. Your enemy the devil prowls around like a roaring lion looking for someone to devour"* (1 Peter 5:8 NIV).

It is God's desire that your spouse turn totally to Him and that your marriage be restored and healed. It is the devil's desire that your spouse be lost eternally and that your marriage be destroyed.

The conflict is that simple. The circumstances particular to your spouse and marital situation are only the particular means of warfare that your enemy has chosen to employ in your case. He knows the weaknesses of each of you. He knows what will wound you the most. The devil doesn't play fair. He kicks you when you are down. He strikes the hardest when you are your weakest. But he is limited in his means of warfare. *"There is no temptation taken you but such as is common to man: but God is faithful, who will not suffer you to be tempted above that ye are able; but will with the temptation make a way to escape"* (1 Corinthians 10:13 KJV). The devil is limited in his weapons. He can only come after you with carnal weapons — things that are common to man. He cannot use supernatural means to war against you. God has promised you a way out with each attack of the enemy.

Scripture, however, has great promises for you regarding your weapons. *"It is true that I am an ordinary, weak human being, but I don't use human plans and methods to win my battles. I use God's mighty weapons, not those made by men, to knock down the devil's strongholds. These weapons can break down every proud argument against God and every wall that can be built to keep men from finding him. With these weapons I can capture rebels and bring them back to God, and change them into men whose hearts' desire is obedience to Christ"* (2 Corinthians 10:3-5 TLB). God has provided you with weapons that are supernatural and mighty to fight against the devil.

The key is to stay in the spirit and fight the battle totally in the spirit. The devil is a master of the flesh. He knows your flesh better than you know it yourself. If you get in the flesh, he will win every time. If you stay in the spirit, you will win every time.

What does it mean to stay in the spirit? Well, your spouse is saying and doing many ungodly things right now. You need to constantly remember that your battle is not with your spouse. Read Ephesians 6:12. You are not warring against flesh and blood. Your spouse is not your enemy, Satan is. So staying in the spirit means that when you see or hear your spouse doing or saying ungodly things you don't react with your flesh. Yelling, scheming, arguing, threatening are all fleshly means of dealing with the problem.

Recognize right now that you are fighting the kingdom of hell for your spouse and your marriage. Staying in the spirit means that you do spiritual warfare against your true enemy, the devil, and you do not war in the flesh against your spouse. Think of your spouse as a hostage or a prisoner of war in the enemy camp. Your spiritual warfare is going to be the means of your spouse's freedom.

Circumstances are the chief weapons of your enemy. One of his greatest tricks is to get your eyes on circumstances and off Jesus. What are you facing today? Is your spouse filing for divorce? Is your spouse in jail? Are you being threatened with a custody battle? Whatever you are facing, it is a circumstance. Do not let it control you. Instead, you begin to turn the tide against it with prayer.

Now this type of warfare is going to take spiritual insight and discernment. It does not mean saying, "Dear God, please bless our marriage. Thank you. Amen." It does mean identifying demonic spirits in operation and taking up your spiritual weapons against them in the name of Jesus. It is an active warfare, not a passive sitting back and waiting.

It is not the purpose of this book to teach you the depths of spiritual warfare that you are going to need. There are many excellent books in Christian book stores that will teach you what you need to know. You may also wish to ask your pastor to recommend some.

It is the purpose of this book, though, to help equip you for the battle ahead. Just before Jesus ascended into heaven, He told His disciples to wait in Jerusalem to be baptized with the Holy Spirit (Acts 1:4,5) He promised them that power would come upon them when this happened. (Acts 1:8). Those to whom He spoke had already been born again when He came to them after His death and resurrection (John 20:22). It was obvious from what is recorded in the first chapter of Acts, though, that Jesus was telling them that there was another, separate experience available to them. Read Acts, chapters 1 and 2.

Do you see the amazing transformation of the people? Those who had been so fearful and had even denied knowing Jesus suddenly became bold and proclaimed the Gospel fearlessly. As the Holy Spirit came upon them in might and power, He confirmed His presence by giving new languages to each who received Him.

Read Romans 8:26,27. When we do not know how to pray, the Holy Spirit knows how to pray the perfect will of God through us.

"For when I pray in a tongue, my spirit prays, but my mind is unfruitful" (1 Corinthians 14:14 NIV). During this time of turmoil in your life, you need to be able to pray with your mind being unfruitful. There are going to be so many circumstances that are going to confuse you. There are going to be so many people giving you advice. You must know what God is saying in each situation. The only way you can do that is for the Holy Spirit to pray God's perfect will for you and your family in each situation.

As you read through the Book of Acts, you will see that the Baptism or Infilling of the Holy Spirit happened over and over again. It was not a one-time experience in the history of the church nor is it reserved by God for just a chosen few. The same power that was available to them then is available to you now. All you need do is ask. (Luke 11:11-13).

If it is your desire for the Holy Spirit to come upon you in might and power right now, pray this prayer:

"Jesus, I have received You as my Lord and Savior. I renounce all works of the enemy that may have been a part of my life. I ask You to baptize me in the Holy Spirit."

Wait upon the Lord as you pray this prayer. Allow the Holy Spirit to fill you to overflowing. Very soon new words will begin to form within you. Remember, they will come from your spirit, not your brain. Do not try to understand or analyze them. Just open your mouth and begin to praise the Lord. Allow the new language that He has given you to begin to flow forth in praise.

You are totally in control of this new language. You can begin praying in it when you desire and stop when you desire. It is not some uncontrollable thing that comes over you. You have the same control over it that you have over speaking in your native language. The difference is this new tongue is a private language between you and God.

You can sing in your new language also. Pick a song that you really love and begin to sing it in your new language. You will not understand what you are saying, but God will. Sing to Him, praise Him, pray to Him. The more you use the language He has given you, the more fluent you will become. Do not be concerned if at first you only have a word or two. The more you use them, the more words will be added.

You will find several things have happened since you have been filled with the Spirit. Scripture will take on a whole new depth for you. You will find you have a greater desire to praise and worship the Lord. You will begin to develop a deeper relationship with the Holy Spirit. He is your teacher (John 14:26) and your comforter (John 16:7). He always lifts up Jesus and He will teach you how to exalt Him in your life. Learn to hear the voice of the Holy Spirit. Through praying in your prayer language (in tongues), He will direct you into God's will for every aspect of your life.

"Lord Jesus, thank You for the Holy Spirit. Thank You for this new depth in my walk with You. Help me to remember daily that my battle is not with flesh and blood. Help me not to react to circumstances, good ones or bad ones, but to just keep my eyes on You.

Holy Spirit, teach me, counsel me, comfort me. I know You are praying the perfect will of God through me as I pray in the new tongue I have received. Help me to discern His will in every area of my life. Teach me to do spiritual warfare against my real enemy, the devil. Amen."

—5—
Blurry Vision

Now that you know who your real enemy is, it is time to learn to love your spouse as God loves your spouse, with agape love, not frail human love.

Romans 2:4 says it is God's kindness (or goodness) that leads us to repentance. God loves us into His kingdom. While we were still sinners Christ died for us (Romans 5:8). Your spouse needs to know the unconditional love of God. No matter what your spouse is doing, God's love has not changed.

If you are self-righteous and judgmental toward your spouse, you give the impression that the God you represent is also that way. That kind of spiritual pride will not draw anyone to the kingdom of God.

Your sin of self righteousness is not smaller in God's eyes than the "big" sin of your spouse. God does not see big and little sin. Sin is sin to God. I have heard people tell me how very much they are praying for their spouse to be born-again and for their marriage to be healed and then I have watched them treat their spouse like dirt. That is not the way God sees them and He will not honor your treating your spouse that way. If you have been doing that, you need to repent.

You need to will to forgive your spouse. You probably do not feel like it right now. You probably will not feel like it for some time. It is what God desires for you to do, though, and is His will for you (Matthew 6:14,15). Line your will up with His and will to forgive your spouse. Release the hurt to the Lord and allow Him to begin to change your heart. The feelings will follow. Don't let them lead.

Begin to see your spouse as God sees your spouse. God has a plan for each one of us -- a **faith vision** that He maintains in His heart waiting for someone on earth to agree with Him for it. When Abraham was willing to take God's word regarding his child and believe right along with God, the promise came to pass. The promise of God materialized in Abraham's son, Isaac.

God has a plan for your spouse. God sees your spouse through supernatural eyes and He wants you to see your spouse the same way. God wants your supernatural vision to be 20/20.

Up until now you have seen what your spouse is like and have accepted that as the reality of the situation. It has not been difficult to see that your spouse and your marriage are not what they should be.

You may also be seeing yourself in a very negative light. Perhaps you are going over again in your mind mistakes that you have made, things that you have done or said that you wish you could now change. You need to begin to see yourself, your spouse, and your marriage as God sees them.

When I was standing for the healing of our marriage, I would do fine as long as Michael was out of the house. I would read the Word, pray in the spirit, praise the Lord, and do spiritual warfare. I would make up my mind that the next time I saw Michael I would show him the unconditional love of God. I would not fight with him, I would stay out of the flesh. Then Michael would walk in the door and say something nasty to me and the fight would be on. In a short time he would leave again shouting something like, "You're never going to change. You'll always be the same. You say Jesus has made a difference in your life. Well, I sure can't see it."

Immediately I would regret my words and actions and repent for being so much in the flesh. I'd ask God to help me to be better next time (if there ever were a next time) and then I'd spend the next two hours crying because I thought for sure I had blown my marriage healing.

One day during a repeat of this activity, the Lord spoke to my heart. He told me the reason I couldn't treat Michael with unconditional love was that I saw him as he was and I reacted to what I saw. He told me His Word had not become revelation to me and I was just quoting it aimlessly.

Read Luke 4:1-13. when the devil tempted Jesus, he chose temptations that would mean something to Him. Jesus was hungry after His long fast, so bread was a real temptation. Jesus had come to take back the kingdoms of the world, so that also was a valid temptation. Jesus had left the glory that was His in heaven to become a servant here on earth (Phil. 2:6-8). The third temptation was also valid in that it challenged who Jesus really was and dared Him to prove it.

In reply to each one of those temptations, Jesus responded with the Word. He didn't agree with Satan nor did He argue with him. Instead Jesus used the Word as a sword (Ephesians 6:17) and fought Satan in the spirit realm. The reason Jesus could do this so successfully was that He knew what the Word of God had to say about each one of those temptations. The Word was His plumb line and He used it to measure everyone and everything.

Do you know how God sees your spouse? The day that the Lord

told me His Word had not become revelation to me, I realized that I did not see Michael as He did. I asked Him to show me Michael from His Word that I could agree with Him. He took me to 1 Timothy 3:2-4. *"Now the overseer ('elder' in King James version) must be above reproach, the husband of but one wife, temperate, self-controlled, respectable, hospitable, able to teach, not given to drunkenness, not violent but gentle, not quarrelsome, not a lover of money. He must manage his own family well and see that his children obey him with proper respect"*(NIV). I have to confess when I first read this scripture, I couldn't believe it. My husband was an alcoholic in adultery. He despised the things of God and mocked me for my beliefs. I read the scripture again and said, "Lord, are we talking about the same man?"

The Lord spoke something to me then that is so important I hope you grasp its depth. He said, "That's how I see him, Marilyn. He is to be a preacher and teacher of the Word. Others are going to be brought to Me by him. You can either agree with the devil that Michael is what you see with your natural eyes or you can agree with My Word and see him with supernatural eyes."

I was stunned. Up until then I had been begging God to somehow drag Michael into the kingdom. I thought if he only could get near a church or hear a Full Gospel Business Men's meeting in one of the restaurants he frequented, he might receive Jesus. In my mind I had always seen Michael just squeaking in. Suddenly I realized how far below God's vision my vision had been. I repented and immediately wrote down that scripture with Michael's name inserted in it. I began to ask God for other scriptures for Michael and I wrote all of them down with Michael's name in them. And then God taught me something else.

He took me to Genesis, Chapter 1, and led me through the account of the creation of the world. Then He said to me, "If I being God must speak in order for things to come to pass, what makes you believe that you can just think them and they will be?"

I realized that when I prayed the Word for Michael I just sat quietly and did it in my head. I began to see that those words had to be spoken forth out loud in order for the promise to come forth. I began that day to pray the Word out loud saying, "Michael is..." I prayed the Word over and over again daily and each time I thought how much God must have been working on Michael out there somewhere. Was he ever going to be a changed man the next time I saw him?

Then the funniest thing happened. One day Michael came in

with the usual provoking greeting. I remember I was standing in the hall looking at him and I thought to myself, "I wonder why he said that. That's not at all like him." Suddenly I realized that the Word of God had become revelation to me. The man I knew Michael to be from God's Word was more real to me than the man who stood before me temporarily bound by the enemy. All the time I thought God was changing Michael, He was changing me! God was working on my heart so that I could see Michael as He saw him.

From that moment on, nothing could change the way I felt about my husband. I could love him with unconditional agape love because I knew who he was in Christ. The words of his mouth and his actions were easily identifiable as the work of the enemy. When he said, "I hate you and wish I'd never met you," I knew that was how Satan felt about me. It sure wasn't the heart of that godly man who was going to preach and teach in the name of the Lord!

There were many even tougher times ahead for us but the enemy couldn't shake me from knowing God's promise for Michael. No matter what the devil threw at me, I could quote, "It is written..." God's Word was revelation to me.

Let God's Word become revelation to you, too. Ask Him to show you how He sees your spouse. Write down those scriptures and speak them forth daily. Let faith come by hearing (Romans 10:17). The more you speak them forth, the more you hear them, the more you will believe what God says.

You need to see yourself as God sees you, too. Whatever you have done wrong in the past was forgiven the minute you repented. Don't let the devil harass you and tell you that you're not good enough to get your marriage healed. The healing of your marriage is based on Jesus' perfection, not yours. All you are responsible for is obedience and repentance when you fail to obey. That is what will bring God's will to pass in your home. Ask God how He sees you also. Write down those scriptures with your name in them. Speak them forth out loud, let your ears hear how God sees His precious child -- you!

"Lord, I thank you for your Word. I thank You that You keep Your Word. Today I agree with what you have to say about my spouse and about me. I agree with Your Word for our marriage and our family. I will not listen to the voice of the enemy any longer. I will agree only with You. Let Your unconditional, agape love flow from me to my spouse. Let _____ see You through the kindness I show in Your name. Amen."

Physical Therapy

Healing is going to take a while. You need to give God all the time He needs to complete the work. Do not become impatient with yourself, just follow His directions and let Him heal you from the inside out.

Give Him all the time He needs to work on your spouse. Don't become anxious and try to hurry things up a bit. Mark 4:26-29 talks about a growing seed. Read it now.

Realize that you are planting seeds of marriage healing. You are sowing good seed to reap a good harvest. Galatians 6:7-9 (NIV) says, *"Do not be deceived: God cannot be mocked. A man reaps what he sows... Let us not become weary in doing good, for at the proper time we will reap a harvest if we do not give up."*

God has a timetable for the seed you have planted. It will come to harvest when it is mature. Each crop has its own timetable. Do not compare your marriage to someone else's. Do not try to harvest your crop before it is ready. Do not demand that things come together before their time. God knows how long it will take to heal your marriage. Leave it in His hands.

You will have well-meaning friends and counselors who will feel that you have waited long enough. They will tell you that if God were going to do something, He would have done it by now. Stand firm on what God has spoken to you. God gives the grace to go through something to the one who is going through it, not to those who are watching. In 2 Corinthians 12:9, the Lord said to Paul, *"My grace is sufficient for you, for my power is made perfect in weakness."* God will not only give you grace to face what you must, but He will also perfect His power in your weakness.

Think of this healing time as a course of physical therapy. When a human body has been injured, it has a tendency to become "stiff" as it heals. The job of the physical therapist is to force the body to move even when it doesn't feel like it. It is painful at times and usually not what the person would do on their own if they were not forced to do it.

You have been wounded. Your marriage has been wounded. Sometimes it seems easier to just stay where you are in your pain and wait for it to go away. God has plan for healing, though, and that plan is going to force you beyond what you would be willing to do on your own. Through this time He is not just healing your marriage, He is also causing growth within you at a rate that probably would not have been achieved without the pain. There will be days when you just wish God would leave you alone and let you just sit in your misery. Just like the skilled physical therapist, however, God is going to help you go beyond your own limits. His plan is to bring a vibrant wholeness and health to your marriage that will reflect His glory. He is not just doing this for you. He has a call upon your lives together in this marriage and He plans to touch many others through the two of you.

If you are standing for the healing of your marriage just for your needs to be met, there will be times when you will be more comfortable just forgetting the whole thing. If, however, you realize there is a greater purpose of God in all of this, you will have the strength and courage to allow God to do what He needs to do even though it hurts.

The time that it took to stand for the healing of our marriage seems very little now in comparison to the joy that God has established in our lives. It seems He has truly redeemed the time and has accomplished more in us and through us in the years since our reconciliation than could have been accomplished had we not given Him those years to heal. The fruit of the years of standing is much greater than the time it took.

Today Michael truly is the godly man that the Lord spoke of years ago. He is born-again, filled with the Holy Spirit and on fire for God. He is a preacher and teacher of the Word and has led many to the Lord just as He said he would. The Lord has established us as a couple in a ministry to marriages and we have watched Him touch thousands of lives through us. God has expanded the ministry world-wide that couples of every nation and tongue might know of His plan for their homes. What a waste it would have been had we let Satan have this marriage.

God has a plan for the two of you also. You have been given an assignment that is yours alone. The victory gained in your home is going to minister to more people than you can imagine.

"Lord Jesus, I give You permission to do what You need to do within me and within my life. I know it will sometimes be painful, but I am willing to let You take me beyond my comfort zone. Mold me, Lord, into Your image. Use me, Lord, for the glory of Your name. And, Father, when our marriage is reconciled and healed, use us as a mighty one-flesh team to take Your love and healing to others. Give me vision now for Your future plan. In Jesus' name, amen."

*M*arriage *M*inistries *I*nternational
(Nova Shalom)

Mike and Marilyn Phillipps are the Founders and International Directors of Marriage Ministries International. Through weekly home meetings, seminars, and church retreats, MMI leadership couples minister to thousands of marriages weekly across the United States and on five other continents. Couples are taught the depth of covenant commitment and given scriptural principles which will resurrect dead marriages, heal wounded ones, and fortify stable marriages in Jesus.

PLEASE SEND INFORMATION:

About believing for the healing of my marriage.

❏ My spouse and I are ❏together ❏separated ❏divorced.

My spouse is ❏willing ❏unwilling to work on our marriage.

❏ About MMI groups.

❏ My spouse and I are willing to work on our marriage together.

❏ About seminars and retreats for couples.

Name _____

Address _____

City _____ State _____ Zip _____

Phone (_____) _____

Mail to: Marriage Ministries International
                PO Box 1040
                Littleton, CO 80160-1040

FOR ADDITIONAL COPIES OF THIS BOOKLET AND OTHER
MATERIALS, SEE THE OTHER SIDE OF THIS SHEET.

 Books

First Aid for a Wounded Marriage
A booklet designed to minister to those whose marriage is troubled and whose spouse is not willing to help get it healed. (Available in English, Portuguese, Spanish, and Afrikaans)
Marilyn Phillips
$2.00

An Alternative to Divorce
The director of Covenant Keepers International offers a Biblical alternative to divorce, including scriptural guidelines for marriage healing.
Marilyn Conrad
$2.00

Faith: Believe It or Not
This book is packed with faith-building accounts from Dave and Bonnie's ministry around the world.
Dave Duell
$5.00

Marriage: Covenant or Contract
A comprehensive study of marriage, divorce, and remarriage in the Church. Learn what the Word really says.
Craig Hill
$3.00

First Aid Kit For A Wounded Marriage
Finally, a marriage version of the familiar household medical box that families run to when someone's hurt. Recognizably packaged kit contains: "First Aid For A Wounded Marriage", Mike & Marilyn's testimony tapes, plus actual "scripture bandaids".
Mike and Marilyn Phillips
$16.00

Whose Report Will You Believe?
In her new release, Marilyn recounts the expectations, crisis, and moments of lonely hopelessness from her own courtship and marriage against a background of God's power and covenant faithfulness. An encouragement to those who are fighting for their marriage without their spouse's cooperation.
Marilyn Phillips
$3.00

	Qty.	Price	Total
		X $2	
		X $2	
		X $5	
		X $3	
		X $16	
		X $3	
Column 1 Total			

Tapes

Keys to Marriage Healing and Growth
Six tape series that includes Mike and Marilyn's testimony, steps to soul healing, sexual healing, and family healing.
Mike and Marilyn Phillipps
$24.00

Understanding One-Flesh
Two tape series that shares God's blueprint for covenant and one-flesh vision.
Mike and Marilyn Phillipps
$10.00

The Third Season
Three tape series based on Isaiah 37:30, examines the time to receive and the time to give. Discover your season.
Mike and Marilyn Phillipps
$12.00

Videos

Fighting for Your Home
2 Hour Video in three segments include their testimony, "1 Samuel 30 - Three Reasons to Stand", and "Pitfalls of Standing."
Mike and Marilyn Phillipps
$15.00

Divorce and Remarriage
An exploration of what Jesus and the Scriptures say about this important subject.
Mike and Marilyn Phillipps
$12.00

	Qty.	Price	Total
		X $24	
		X $10	
		X $12	
		X $15	
		X $12	
Column 2 Total			
Column 1 Total			
Sub Total			
Postage & Handling			
TOTAL ENCLOSED			

Postage & Handling

On orders of	add
$1.00 - $4.00	$1.00
$4.01 - $10.00	$1.50
$10.01 - $30.00	$2.00
$30.01 or more	$3.00

Name	
Address	
City	State	Zip
Phone ( )	

Mail to:
Marriage Ministries International
PO Box 1040
Littleton, CO 80160-1040
(303) 730-3333

Check#	
Visa	MasterCard
Card #	
Expires	
Signature	

Payment Must Accompany Order

US Funds Only Please